After the fl

Story by Jenny Giles

Illustrated by Isabel Lowe

"The flood is over," said Mom.
"We can start cleaning up now."

"Our car is all muddy,"
said Rachel.

Dad said,
"I will have to hose it down."

Rachel and Sam
ran up the steps with Mom.

They went into the kitchen.
"Oh good," said Mom.
"The flood didn't come up here,
and the phone
is working again."

"Spot's going down
 to the playroom," said Sam.

"Stop him," said Mom.
"It will be all muddy down there."

"Spot!" called Sam. "Spot!
 Come back up here!"

But Spot ran all the way down the stairs to the playroom. He ran around and around on the muddy floor.

"Woof," he barked. "Woof! Woof!"

"Spot! Come here!" called Sam.

Spot ran
over to Sam.
He jumped
up on him,
and Sam fell over.

Rachel laughed.

"You are
so muddy,"
she said.
Then Spot
jumped up
on Rachel,
and she
fell over, too.

Sam and Rachel
laughed and laughed.
"Woof! Woof!" barked Spot.

Mom came down the stairs.
"I'm going to start cleaning now,"
she said.

She saw a muddy Sam
and a muddy Rachel
and a muddy Spot.

"Oh **no**!" said Mom.
"Off you go, outside!
Dad can hose you down, too."

"I like
    cleaning up,"
said Rachel.

"Yes!"
    laughed Sam.
"It's fun!"